Knowledge Reduces Fear

A RESOURCE FOR END OF LIFE EDUCATION

We, as a society, know very little about dying and death. What we do know has been influenced by movies and television programs that provide a dramatized version of death, NOT the real thing. This misinformation leaves us woefully unprepared, uninformed and full of fear.

I believe that knowledge reduces fear which is why I have dedicated my life to educating the public about the dying process. I hope that the knowledge shared in this collection of some of my most popular blog posts will help you overcome your own fear of death. I invite you to replace that fear with an understanding of the normal, natural way people die.

Just as the little chick works hard to get out of its shell, we humans labor to get out of our bodies. Understanding this labor takes away some of the fear we bring to the bedside of someone who is dying.

Blessings,

Barbara

Barbara Karnes, RN writes articles, answers questions and addresses concerns about end of life care on her award winning weekly blog - *Something to Think About: A Blog on End of Life*. Visit her website **bkbooks.com** to follow her blog and for more information about her work.

Table of Contents

Section I - Dynamics of Dying
- Barbara's Hospice Beginning ... 1
- Death: Gradual or Fast / A Better Place ... 2
- Beware of Life Expectancy Numbers / Beware of Numbers Part II ... 3
- The Gift of Time / Other People Die ... 4
- We Know When We Are Dying / Patterns of Living and Dying ... 5
- Personal Approaches to Dying / Window of Control ... 6
- What Does Death Look Like? ... 7

Section II - Questions From Barbara's Blog
- Personality Changes ... 8
- Aggression and Rejection: How to Cope? ... 9
- When Do We Talk About End of Life? / How Do You Talk About End of Life? ... 10
- Denial ... 11
- How Does Disease Happen? ... 12
- How Long Do I Have to Live? / Life is a Terminal Illness ... 13
- What Happens When We Die? ... 14

Section III - Hospice
- When to Call Hospice / What Do You Do When a Hospice Patient Improves? ... 15
- Is the Process of Dying Different for the Elderly? ... 16
- Where to Die ... 17
- The Emperor's New Clothes ... 18

Section IV - Medical Terminology
- Life Sustaining vs. Comfort Care ... 19
- Terminal Secretions (Death Rattle) ... 21
- Terminal Restlessness / Vomiting ... 22
- Palliative Sedation ... 23
- Advance Directives: Afraid to Talk About Dying ... 24
- Full Code vs. No Code ... 25

Section V - Grief
- Normal Grief ... 26
- Grief and Suicide ... 27
- Grieving and Dementia ... 28
- Family and Grief / Grief and the Holidays ... 29
- Time to Say Goodbye ... 30

Section I: Dynamics of Dying

Barbara's Hospice Beginning

How did I begin in hospice? In 1981 there was one hospice in Kansas City and that hospice was Hospice Care of Mid America. It was an all volunteer hospice as were most hospices at that time and its only funding was from donations. They were taking a big step and looking to pay an RN to provide patient care.

I had just moved to Kansas from Nebraska and was looking to make friends. I attended a Comparative Religion class at a local Unitarian Church thinking I would meet like-minded people. Here is where my belief that there are no coincidences and all is Divine Order comes through for me. There, in the class, was the Volunteer Coordinator of Hospice Care of Mid America. We began talking about hospice and my interest in this budding new concept for end of life care. After much talk and a few classes later he suggested I talk with the Director of Hospice Care of Mid America and apply for the RN position. I was not ready for the full time job but after meeting with the Director, I said I would volunteer twenty hours a week to assist the RN they would hire.

Jody Gyulay, Ph.D, RN and I began seeing patients in 1981. Four months after volunteering I became part of the paid staff. Together with Kevin Flattery, Dennis Henderson, Sister Mary Shields, and Paxton Small, Ph.D, Jody and I helped mold and grow that hospice.

There were no payment sources other than donations, no "How To" manuals on providing patient care, no medical supplies, and no new medical equipment. We used bed pads made out of newspapers covered in old sheets, mayonnaise jars for urinals, Udder Ointment for skin care, old hospital beds, and donated wheelchairs and walkers. What we lacked in knowledge and supplies we made up for with time and presence. We learned how people died by being with them. For hours and hours we'd sit at a bedside, supporting a family, guiding and nurturing them as we all held vigil for their loved one. We learned how scared families were by listening to them. We learned that eating decreases months before death arrives, that sleep increases, withdrawal is normal, and that pain comes from disease not from dying. We learned how breathing changes and a face looks as the last breath is drawn.

My time at Hospice Care of Mid America was a time of pioneering. There weren't workshops or books on end of life to teach us how to provide care. There were no protocols or guidelines, no schools to attend, no certifications to be obtained. We literally faced whatever was presented and acted in the direction our hearts, instincts, and common sense told us to go. Out of those experiences came knowledge and growth not found before. In fact, the reason why I wrote *Gone From My Sight* at that time was because there was no written information on end of life care for professionals let alone for families.

Eventually I became Patient Care Coordinator and later Executive Director of Hospice Care of Mid America. Our census grew as knowledge of hospice became known. I will always remember and cherish those learning, early days as our Camelot period. Care not encumbered with regulations, unnecessary medical procedures and intervention, or reimbursement issues. Care truly directed by a vision and a passion, that ideal of providing services and support based on quality of living and quality of dying.

Death: Gradual or Fast

There are really just two ways to die: fast or gradual.
- Fast death occurs quickly by way of an accident, a heart attack, a stroke, or suicide. A person is alive one minute and dead the next.
- Gradual death occurs in two ways: old age or disease. Gradual death has a process to it. That process begins months before death from disease and years before death from old age with no disease. The only difference between gradual death from old age and gradual death from disease is that someone who is old with no disease occurring in their body will take longer: years instead of months and months instead of weeks.

Everyone, whether dying quickly or gradually, will do the same things in the days to hours before death.

Fast death is unexpected, it just happens. Gradual death has a process, follows a time line. The time line gives us the ability to finish our business and say our goodbyes.

Gradual death is a gift of opportunity.

A Better Place

Most religions of the world teach us that when we are dead we are in a better place. I add to that being dead is easy while being alive is very hard. That said, why do we have such a hard time letting a loved one die when treatment is not working, when extraordinary measures are not producing desired results, when quality of life becomes a question vs. just breathing or having machines facilitate breath.

It will never be "okay" for someone we care about to die, to leave us. We will always want those we care about to stay in our lives. The thing we need to remember is that everyone dies. We will all lose someone we love and want with us. That is life. The question then becomes can we get ourselves to a place where we understand that now is the time that our loved one is going to leave us. Can we get to a place of accepting not that it is okay to die but that this is the time it is going to happen? Can we put our own feelings of loss and abandonment aside and think unselfishly? Can we put ourselves in the position of the person we care about and say to ourselves "Would I want to be like this? Is this how I would want to die?" If the answer is no, and it probably will be, then make the tough decisions. Stay by the bed side, say your goodbyes, and remember they are in a better place than we are.

Beware of Life Expectancy Numbers

Beware of anyone who puts a number on how long someone has to live. There are so many factors that affect the time of our gradual death that the closest anyone can get to determining how long the dying process will take is months, weeks, days, or hours. Numbers don't work when they are based only on lab reports and disease markers. The medical findings contribute to a prognosis but the personality of the person will affect the actual time of death.

There are several important factors affecting the amount of time in which we die a gradual death that the medical model does not take into account:
- Because we deal with the challenge of dying in the same way we have dealt with other challenges in our life –that affects how long our experience is going to be.
- Because our personality doesn't change but actually intensifies its characteristics –that affects how long our experience is going to be.
- Because we have limited control over the exact time that we die – that affects how long our experience is going to be.

To get a gauge of how long someone is going to live once they have been told they can't be fixed we need to closely examine these three things: how they have met other challenges in their life; the kind of personality they have (active, passive, controlling, argumentative, easy going, protective), and to acknowledge that they have a small amount of control over the exact moment they take their last breath.

Beware of Numbers Part II

When medical professionals place a number on how long someone has to live they are doing that person a disservice. Because people don't have accurate role models on what it is like to die most people think they are going to be alive one minute and dead the next. We don't know that there is a process. Imagine the fear of waking up every morning and wondering if you are going to die that day. Whenever I think that is happening to a person with a life threatening illness I respond, "If you can ask yourself, 'Am I going to die today?' then you are probably not. The day that you die you won't ask and you won't care." Think of the fear that simple statement reduces.

I believe we have the right to be told about our disease, its progression, the options of care, and the probability of being cured vs. our life prolonged. If the only option is prolonged life, what kind of quality can be expected. We have the right to be told if we can't be fixed. It gives us an opportunity to live until we die in a manner of our own choice based on fact. But no one can be so specific as to say exactly how long someone has to live. There are too many personal variables. There is limited control over the time that we die.

The Gift of Time

I, Barbara, am not afraid of being dead. I have a belief system that says "When you are dead you are in a better place." I also think being dead is easy and being alive is hard work. So I am not afraid of being dead but I am really nervous about the time in my life from right now until when I am dead. I am actually more afraid of dying than I am of being dead.

Recognizing this part of myself I thought if God, which is what I call my Higher Power, were to say to me, "You are going to die like this (on a particular day, at a particular time and this is how you are going to die)," I would relax. I would put aside my fears of what kind of scary, unexpected death life has in store for me and live a freer life. When a physician says, "I can't fix you. Go home. Put your affairs in order. You are going to die sometime soon," that message is the same as my fantasy. You are being told when you are going to die. Yet most often people stop really living and concentrate on their life ending. Since we are all going to die someday, being told you can't be fixed could be considered a gift. A gift of time to say and an opportunity to do those things that are important.

Other People Die!

Most people, when they have been told they can't be fixed, associate that as a statement of failure: the enemy (death) has not been conquered. The reality is we are all going to die someday. It is the only guarantee life offers. But we each think in our mind that it is other people who die. I'm not going to die and neither is anyone close to me. Other people die! We cannot comprehend ourselves as dead. We can even talk about our not being able to be fixed but deep inside we really don't believe it. We think, "The diagnosis was a mistake," "There will be a cure," or "There will be a miracle." It is just too much for the mind to see ourselves as being dead.

In the months before a gradual death we really don't believe death will happen to us or to those we love. In the days to weeks before gradual death occurs a person realizes, at last, that they are dying. Because we live inside of our bodies, there comes a point when no one has to tell us we are dying. We know it on some level though we may not share that knowledge with others. If asked we may deny it but deep, deep down we know it: We are dying. This is why the "Don't tell Mom" theory doesn't work, she knows. Not telling her and not talking about this huge challenge in both of your lives results in loneliness and isolation. Everyone is alone and scared. If you talk about what life is offering, even when it's death, you may still be scared and of course very sad but no one will be alone.

We Know When We Are Dying

Question: Is it possible to recognize the signs of approaching death in the months before an undiagnosed person dies from an illness?

That is an interesting question and there are so many variables that there is no one answer. Here are some ideas to consider: Some people, who appear healthy with no evidence of disease, begin the dying process and go through the stages of dying without ever being diagnosed with a life threatening disease. They die and everyone is surprised. If you had asked them "are you sick" some might have said "yes," others may have said "no." Some may just have been in denial while others may have known how serious it was and just chose to do nothing.

Another possibility is a person was healthy and well, got an illness, and even though they weren't "supposed" to die from the illness, they did. In that case they would not have entered the dying process before actual death.

While individual differences may be seen in the time of days to weeks before death, everyone who is dying will have the signs of approaching death that occur hours to minutes before death. Even the person dying from being hit by a car, a person I would say is having a fast death, will show the signs of hours to minutes before death. In the last moments of life we all die similarly.

Often in hindsight we can see that indeed the person did show signs of approaching death months before actual death occurred. Eating decreased, sleeping increased, and they withdrew from those around them. That would tell us the body had the disease long before it was (if ever) diagnosed.

In our personal situations we may never have an answer to the question did the person know they were dying or had the dying process started months earlier. What I suspect is that at some time before we die we know that the moment has come. That knowledge may become real to us weeks, days, hours or minutes before death but there is a moment when without a doubt we know –this is what dying is like.

Patterns of Living and Dying

We will meet the challenge of a gradual death in the same manner we have met other challenges in our life. Dying a gradual death is just one more challenge in living—a big one, maybe the biggest of our whole life, but another life experience nevertheless.

If we are a controlling person we will control this experience. If we run away from our challenges, we will stay in denial. If we are secretive we may not tell others what we are thinking or feeling. If we are organized we will make sure our affairs are in order.

Look at how a person lived their life and they will follow that same pattern in their dying a gradual death.

Personal Approaches to Dying

When we begin the gradual dying process our personality doesn't change, it intensifies. If we are an angry person we will get angrier. If we are a gentle personality we will become even softer. You would think we would become more thoughtful about life and its meaning and more religious or spiritual but generally we don't. We just continue down life's path in the same direction we always have, a bit more frightened, a bit more nervous maybe but basically just a sicker version of who we have always been. If I have been active all of my life I will push myself to keep going. If I have been passive I will succumb to the temptation to be a couch potato, a complainer will get out the microphone, a loner will withdraw even more.

Learn about how a person has lived their life and you will better understand how they will approach their death.

Window of Control

If you are with someone at the moment they take their last breath you are with them because they want you there. If you are not with someone at the moment they died, and you tried very hard to be with them, then they showed their love for you by protecting you from that moment. It sounds strange, but the person who is dying is the one who has a limited amount of control over the moment that they die—not the loved one who is attending to them.

We die a gradual death according to our personality and if that personality is protective then we may protect a person we care about by dying when they are not in the room. We tend to believe that death just happens but, as I have said, gradual death has recognizable dynamics with a process to it. Part of that process is a small window of control over the time that we actually die.

We have enough control to wait until a child, even an adult child, leaves the room. We have enough control to wait until a special person arrives to be with us. I know this seems foreign but there is self-determination over the time that we die, limited, but more than most of us assume. We can take comfort in this knowledge. We can let go of guilty feelings and accept the gift our loved one has given us: presence at the moment of death or protection from it--whichever the dying person thought best.

What Does Death Look Like?

When my mother was a little girl she sat in a rocking chair, accidentally rocked on a kitten, and killed it. It was not instantly dead but her no-nonsense father told her to bury it. Without recounting the entire story, as the result of this horrible first experience with death, she was terrified of death from that day forward. She passed on that terror to all of her children. When I was in my thirties my grandfather died and I would not go to the visitation for the traditional viewing because I was scared to see the body. Where did that fear come from? Some of it came from my mother, of course, it was what I had learned.

Most of us bring our fears, our childhood experiences, our culture, our belief systems, our role models, and our stereotypes to the bedside of the dying and the dead. Wherever our fears have come from they are generally irrational and emotional. The purpose of this article is to help add some reality to our preconceived ideas of death. In this way we can counteract our fears with knowledge---and knowledge reduces fear.

What does a dying person look like in the hours to minutes before death? Generally they are non responsive, their eyes are partially open, the skin color is palish often with a yellowish or bluish tint, and the skin is cool to cold to the touch. Sometimes the eyes will tear, or you will see just one or two tears in an eye. The person will probably pee or stool as a last release. Their breathing is very slow and often changes to look like a fish breathes with their mouth opening and closing. The breathing gets slower and slower and slower until there are two or three long spaced out breaths. You will think there isn't going to be another breath, and then there is, which startles everyone. Finally there are no more breaths and the physical life is gone.

With death the body looks the same as it did just a few minutes before but now there is no movement. There are no sounds---all is quiet--unless you move the body. If you turn the body (when you are giving a final bath) the body may make sounds like gurgles or rasps. Those momentary sounds are not life. They are just the body fluids rearranging.

Rigor mortis (body stiffness) begins to occur two to six hours after death. If the body is not embalmed, say for a home funeral, it will begin to relax again after about thirty-six hours. The body temperature begins dropping over a period of hours and will feel cold after about eight hours.

A person generally dies with their eyes partially open. If you try to close the eyes they will slowly open again. That is normal. It is only in the movies that the eye lids stay shut.

There is nothing bad or scary about a dead body. It is only an empty shell, a deserted vehicle. The "driver," that essence that makes us who we are, is gone. You can feel the emptiness, you can see the emptiness. Life is gone.

(*The Eleventh Hour* has a detailed explanation of what happens in the days to hours before a gradual death.)

Section II: Questions from the Blog

Personality Changes

Question: Do you care to comment more in depth on personality changes as people approach death? You spoke of how we all wear faces; I assume that as the effort and intensity involved in approaching death increases, a person loses the desire and or energy to maintain a "public face." You also spoke about how sometimes what we see at the end of life is not the true person, but a disease-distorted self. How do we know which is which? And does it matter? Should we just write off all unpleasant personality changes as the consequence of the diseases (medications)?

I think the key to addressing the questions above is realizing that we die the way we have lived. The personality doesn't change, it intensifies, so if we were a "game player" (and we all are, it's just a matter of degree) then we will continue playing the games we are familiar with---denial, little girl, macho man, victim, aggressor, controller, etc. As we begin to withdraw from the world around us, on the continuum of gradual death, we have less energy to interact with others and we care less about what is happening (what people are saying, thinking, and doing) so the games decrease. There just isn't the desire to communicate with others. The life work has gone inward so there is less concern about what is occurring outward.

As far as what I think we should "write off?"----All of it. Now is the time to put judgements and expectations aside and be in the moment. A person we care about is leaving this world. What they are experiencing is how they are leaving. They are doing it in their own unique way just as they lived their life in their own unique way. This is their final experience in the adventure we call life. Our role (whoever is present during this final journey whether it is family, friends, or health care professionals) is first of all to see that the patient is free of physical pain (if pain has been a part of the disease process, keep medicating, if not a part of the disease process, then pain is not likely to be present as death approaches). This includes making sure that they are in a clean dry bed and safe from physical harm (falling out of bed or otherwise hurting themselves). We get to use this opportunity to express our love and appreciation. It is time to say our goodbyes.

People with unpleasant personalities while living will still have unpleasant personalities while dying. It is just that the closer to death they get, the less energy they will have to express themselves. You won't change them now. In fact, now, in the months before death, we need to let go of all those things we wish we had or thought we needed in our relationship from our mother, father, husband, wife, or children (whoever it is that we are dealing with losing) but didn't get. It is too late. The person who is dying doesn't have the energy or the inclination to address those issues. At this time I recommend we give what it is that we wanted. Turn the tables and give what you didn't get but still need. Generally, it is love and attention that we want so desperately and find so lacking. Actually, a person doesn't have to be dying for you to try this. Give what you want. It might surprise you.

Aggression, Rejection - How to Cope?

Question: What to do when a dying daughter who was had radiation treatment to the brain and turns on you. Won't let me see her. Sends her husband to tell me hateful things, that aren't true. Never the less I sent her a note of apology for my meddling, as she put it. I had only asked for her pastor to drop in on her. Big mistake on my part. They have no children. She has been the most generous loving daughter until now. I am devastated.

I can't think of greater heartfelt pain than facing the death of a child and then adding to that pain rejection while she is still living. Your heart must be screaming. Any words I offer will not ease your sense of loss, now, or after she is gone. I can only offer an idea to help your understanding so you will not take what is occurring personally.

The brain is our delicate life line. It processes everything. It is so important to life that the hard bone of the skull protects it to keep it safe. When disease and/or treatment for that disease (radiation) gets inside the skull's protection everything changes. The balance is changed. What we know, think, believe, how we react, how we feel, how we move can all be altered. In the case of your daughter her personality has changed. Your job now is to remind yourself that what you are seeing and hearing from your daughter is the disease talking, feeling, and reacting, not your beloved child. It is the disease! Hard to remember and respond to but very important to remember.

What to do? Love her, humor her, be there for her in presence without opinions. Words, happenings, disagreements, opinions, even memories have little place now. Do whatever you need to do to be with her, to spend time with her. No arguments, no "I am right, you are wrong." There isn't time or room for that kind of behavior. You are her mom and love her, that is all that matters now. Talk with her husband, show him this email if it will help. Get him to understand your need to be with her as much as possible.

My blessings to you during the most challenging time of your life.

When Do We Talk About End of Life Issues With Others?

Right now, while we are healthy and our thoughts are not clouded with fear. Right now we can make decisions of how we want to live until we are dead. If we wait and do not talk about and write out our intentions, when that information is needed, someone else will be making the decisions of how our life and death will unfold. Family, significant others, doctors, and medical staff will all be making decisions based on their own agendas. The result of their decisions may not be how we intended to live our final days.

Today, while we are well, we can set the stage for how our final days will unfold. Remember, if we don't make our wishes known now the chances of our being physically able to make them known when we need to are very slim. Someone else will be speaking for us.

Google Advanced Directives for numerous websites that offer information and forms to download. Explain your choices and the forms to your family, have discussions, share feelings, then let them know where you are keeping the form. Give a copy to your physician, tell him or her your thoughts and wishes.

You have taken responsibility for your future.

How Do You Talk About End of Life?

Each person is unique so there is no sure formula for when to talk about end of life issues but here are some ideas to consider:

Everyone has the right to be told they can't be fixed. What they do with that information is their choice. Most people will react the same way they have reacted to every other challenge in their life.

I find it sad when no one will be "real" with a person who is facing the end of their life. Most of us are uncomfortable talking about or even acknowledging decline and the evidence of approaching death. The closeness of our relationship will determine how openly we discuss end of life with a person. If we are close to the person we need to look for an opportunity to have an open discussion. This is not a time for games that all is going to be okay, "we are going to beat this enemy," instead it is time to talk about love and memories.

If you are part of a family dealing with the challenge of a loved one dying you can and should begin a conversation with other family members at any point from diagnosis on. Bring out the possibilities and discuss them. Actually, we should all have these kinds of conversations before we are faced with them.

If a casual friend, neighbor, or member of your religious, civic, or social organization is dealing with a life threatening illness you probably want to wait until they begin a conversation about their life situation. If anyone opens the conversation door don't hesitate to begin listening and offering information. Sometimes it is easier to talk about these matters with someone not as close to us as family.

Denial

Question: Is there anything a person can do to help family members break through denial? Boy, is it unpleasant to be the truth-teller to a person who isn't ready to hear it! Should we just allow others to drift in denial? Should we leave it up to "professionals" to deliver the hard, unpleasant truths?

There are several questions here and I will start with the last one. Yes, professionals, and by that I mean physicians, need to be the first to explain to a patient/ family that a person cannot be fixed or that a point has been reached where the likelihood of a cure and a return to normal life is probably not going to happen. A patient/family needs to hear from their doctor that the dying process has begun.

Physicians are the front runners because they order and oversee the tests, the procedures, and the treatments. A non-physician does not have the credibility of a physician to say that a condition can't be fixed. Once that information has been given and understood, the door is open to discussion by others.

My approach has been that once a person has been told that they can't be fixed if they choose to be in denial then so be it. It is not up to me, as a non-physician professional or lay person, to insist they talk about their feelings. They will face this final challenge in the same way they have faced any other challenge in their life. If they choose not to deal with it, I would not force the issue. However, that said, I won't "play the denial game" with anyone by lying about their prognosis if the subject comes up. I believe it is important to always be gentle and truthful. Generally a person will ask questions when they are ready to hear the answers. At that time they deserve the truth as we know it.

I don't like to leave families in denial about approaching death. As a non-physician end of life professional I would try to gently guide significant others into understanding where a person is in the dying process, what they can expect to happen, and what they can do to support the people they care about. Because knowledge reduces fear, and family and significant others are frightened about what the future now holds for them, most are open to guidance and information. For those who are not open I will still gently tell them the information I feel I need to impart. They don't have to believe me. I can only hope that at some point in this process the information I have given them will surface.

Tensions often develop when family dynamics are such that some members are understanding that death is approaching and others are in denial. It is sad to see the family balance disrupted during a time when they need each other so much.

As friends, neighbors, members of shared religious affiliations, even hospice volunteers, I feel it is not our responsibility to address a family or a patient's denial. This is their life experience. They will meet the challenge as best they can. Be a presence, a support person, a listener. Don't lie if asked what you think, but remember, it is not our place to offer an unsolicited opinion about what is happening.

Denial occurs because we just can't face the reality of a situation. It hurts too much. It is too frightening. It is not productive to insist someone believe what they are not ready to process. It is not productive because there is no way you can make a person believe something, even with rational proof. The proof will be in however the situation unfolds. Time will hold the proof and then the consequences of our denial will be lived. And isn't that what life is about--choices, consequences, and lessons learned?

How Disease Happens

Question: Can you talk about dis-ease and how we bring this upon ourselves?

Another great controversial question. Although there is more and more research which points to stress being related to physical disease, to stress lowering the immune system which in turn leads to disease, I think the majority of people believe that disease just happens. We catch germs, viruses, or cells go rogue. Disease just happens because of poor life style choices in relation to nutrition, exercise, smoking, and alcohol to name just a few.

I am going to suggest that disease can manifest in our lives as the result of dis-ease on levels other than the physical. I think it is easier to explain using examples: a person retires after thirty years of work. This person's idea of self worth comes from their job and the recognition and satisfaction it has brought. Now they are home, no idea of how to enjoy life, to fill their days, and so they find no purpose now to being alive. They don't know how to live other than through their job. Soon an illness develops---the dis-ease in their life has found an outlet - the physical body.

Grieving is a good example of dis-ease manifesting. Men in particular have a hard time with this as they have been taught not to show or express their emotions. If those emotions are held in, not even acknowledged, those sorrowful emotions will come out somewhere; in anger, in alcohol, in illness. The dis-ease eventually reaches the physical body.

I'm not saying all illness is the result of dis-ease in the personality or life but I am saying I think it is worth considering that imbalance in our life can lead to physical illness. That illness isn't all about germs, viruses, and cancer cells but about the body's receptivity to their invasion. Our mental and emotional sense of well being has a healing property in itself.

On a personal note I know my body reacts negatively to worry and fear. The times I have been the sickest are the times I had something occur in my life that caused me great concern, dis-ease. Now, when I experience a very unsettling happening, I remind myself that nothing can ever happen to me or someone I care about that is worth getting sick over. That thought helps me put life's challenges into perspective.

How Long Do I Have to Live?

Question: I have been diagnosed terminally ill with lung cancer and liver cancer. I am not at this moment yet, but wonder, how long?

No one can be specific as to how long someone has to live. We can recognize that a cure is not possible but can't put numbers on the length of life.

Each person's disease process will unfold differently depending on our personality and how we deal with life challenges. As the dying process begins the desire to eat decreases, the need to sleep increases, and our interest in the happenings around us decreases. My booklet, Gone From My Sight: The Dying Experience, explains the unfolding process that occurs months before death actually arrives.

No one knows how long someone has to live but think about this: Life is a terminal illness. We begin dying from the moment we are born. It is just that someone in an unhealthy body is reminded everyday that they are not going to live forever. Someone in a "healthy" body (and who knows if they are truly healthy?) lives under the illusion that they are going to live forever and often wastes this gift of life.

If there are just two ways to die, gradual or fast, then dying from a disease, gradually, is a gift: a gift of time. It gives us the opportunity to do and say what we want and need to do and say before we leave those people who are important to us. My booklet, A Time to Live: Living with a Life-Threatening Illness, gives guidance on how to live with a life-threatening illness until death comes.

You asked a difficult question. It took courage to reach out for answers and direction. I don't have enough information about your illness to be more specific. Talk with your physician, ask if a referral to hospice is timely. We tend to think hospice is for the dying. If that were the case we would all qualify for hospice. Hospice is for those people living with a life-threatening illness. Hospice helps people live until death arrives.

Life is a Terminal Illness

From the moment we are born we begin to die. We are born, we experience, and then we die. All the space between birth and death is living yet we tend to segregate out our final experience as different from all that has preceded it. Really, the part of our life that is associated with dying, that final challenge we will all be presented with whether it is a fast or gradual death, will be met in the same way we have dealt with any other challenge in our life. How we face our impending death can be the time we do our finest work or our most terrifying challenge. The experience of dying a gradual death is an important, integral part of each life. It is an opportunity to write our final chapter, to define the ending of our story.

What Happens When We Die?

Question: What happens when we die and do you (Barbara) believe in reincarnation?

I'm going to interpret the question to be asking what happens at the moment of death rather than what happens after we are dead.

What happens when we die is a question people have been asking literally forever. I don't know what happens when we die. I've never had a near-death experience and I'm still living. I can only share with you what I have come to believe as the result of being around dying and death for so many years and the reading and research I have done.

Years ago I attended a Kenneth Ring weekend workshop of people who have had near-death experiences. One hundred or so people shared of being pronounced clinically dead and revived to tell their story. Kenneth started an organization to support people who have had near death experiences.

Dr. Raymond Moody wrote the book, "Life After Life" in 1975 describing his experience as a heart surgeon with patients he revived and their story of "being dead." He now has a web site addressing and teaching about near death experiences.

Today we have Eben Alexander, a neurosurgeon, sharing his near death experience in "Proof of Heaven." Raymond Moody, Kenneth Ring, and Eben Alexander are just three of many resources addressing near-death experiences.

Consistent in near-death experience stories are the following. Some people experience all, most people recall some:
- A light brighter than the sun
- A sense of moving through a tunnel toward a light
- A feeling of bliss, love, and joy
- A presence offering guidance
- Seeing people that have already died
- Understanding the motives of your actions through a life review
- Observing the activities occurring outside of your physical body

In my workshops I talk about all of us being afraid to die yet frequently I will have someone tell me about their near-death experience and that as a result of that experience they are not afraid to die--because they have and know there is nothing to fear. It is estimated that millions of people have had these kind of near-death experiences. Aren't these many people telling us what it is like to die? I believe they are.

Now to the question of do I believe in reincarnation. To me the concept of reincarnation falls under the category of a personal religious belief. A long time ago I made it my policy to stay away from public discussions on politics and religion. Both areas are emotionally charged. I don't want to have my message about end of life care obscured by someone disagreeing with my political or spiritual beliefs. So thank you for your interest, but I respectfully decline to comment in this format.

Section III: Hospice

When to Call Hospice

Many physicians are reluctant to recommend hospice. It is sad and confusing why they would not give their patients the guidance and comfort that trained hospice professionals can offer. Maybe this reluctance to refer has to do with seeing death as a failure, maybe it is just ignorance as to the true value of hospice. It is perfectly acceptable to ask a physician for a hospice referral. If the signs are there, get the referral and let a hospice professional determine if hospice is appropriate. Three things I look for to tell me if it is time for hospice: 1) the patient's condition is deteriorating in spite of the treatment that is being given; 2) You look at the person and say to yourself (and we have all done this but often not wanted to admit it) this person is not going to be here next year at this time; and 3) the family and/or significant others are having difficulty coping with the seriousness of their loved one's condition.

We generally give people more time than they have. I know it is scary to think of using hospice. It says death will happen soon. But hospice offers so much guidance and support to families that it is in our best interest to at least ask for an informational visit. A hospice referral is a win/win. You win if they say it is too soon and you are not appropriate for hospice care (because you can stop living in fear wondering if you should have called), or you win by coming onto the hospice program and getting much needed guidance, information, and support.

Sometimes patients rally once they are with hospice care. I think it is because hospice is the expert in pain management and comfort care and brings that to the patient and family. Everybody begins to relax a little. You feel less alone, less isolated, and have more knowledge about what happens as death approaches.

I know people think of hospice as caring for those people who are dying but remember we are all dying. Hospice guides and supports people who are in the final act of living.

What Do You Do When A Hospice Patient Improves?

Every so often a person comes onto the hospice program and their condition improves. When a person's condition stabilizes hospice takes them off the program until they begin to decline again. How great is that?

I think one of the reasons people are so hesitant to enter the hospice program is because by doing so they have to acknowledge that death is approaching. We have to let go of the idea that other people die but certainly not me or anyone close to me. Hospice is known to care for people who are dying. Actually, hospice cares for people who are LIVING their final challenge. If people would come on to the hospice program earlier there would be more people "graduating" from the program to live a bit longer, a bit more comfortably.

How does that improvement work? A person may have been in pain from their disease progression and hospice, being the expert in pain and comfort management, addresses the pain and reduces it. Life looks better, is easier, and their condition stabilizes. Hospice care involves nutritional recommendations, emotional support for patient and family, and generally neutralizes the fear that people have surrounding approaching death. Everyone relaxes a little and the patient's condition stabilizes.

When hospice care enters a family's experience that family is no longer alone. There is support during one of the biggest challenges in life. Some people do stabilize for a while when they enter the hospice program. Truthfully, most don't. Most people continue their decline.

Is the Process of Dying Different for the Elderly?

Question: Write something to the living who are young and dying. Signs of what are to come etc...

I put these two questions together even though they came from different sources because the answers relate to each other.

First, there is no difference for a young person dying from disease and an elderly person dying from disease. People dying from disease whether old or young go through the same process. An elderly person with no disease actually goes through the same dying process as someone with a disease, only it takes the healthy, elderly person longer--years instead of months, months instead of weeks. When it comes down to days, hours, and minutes, we all die in the same time frame.

As for the "signs of what is to come" for someone who is young and dying, those signs are also the same for everyone, young and old. People dying from disease or old age, even animals, go through the same process and experience the same challenges. Some people and animals will show all the signs of approaching death, some will show none, but most people and animals will be affected in the following three areas: eating will decrease over a period of several months, sleeping will increase over those same months, and they withdraw from outside interests and become focused inward.

A gradual death, versus a fast death (caused by a heart attack, accident, or suicide), has a normal, natural process to it. It also presents us with the gift of time to do and say those things which are important to us. No matter our age, when we are presented with an unfixable health condition and the idea that we are going to live forever is taken away, more than ever we need to concentrate on living. Our gift is in the knowledge that the present is where truth lies, only the present is real (the past is a memory, the future an idea). We need to live in the present, to make each day worth trading for a day of our life. Isn't that how everybody, healthy or unhealthy, needs to be living?

Where To Die

Question: Talk about dying at home, in the hospital, or in a hospice care facility.

I think it is fair to say that most people, given the choice, would like to die at home, in their own bed, with those people they care about the most close to them, and I'll even throw in that they'd prefer to have their dog or cat on the bed. That seems like the ideal way to say goodbye.

Today that is the least likely place we die. WHY! Several reasons:

1) Most of us don't plan ahead for our dying. As the result, those people closest to us, who are left making decisions when we can't, don't know what we want.

2) It is hard work to care for the dying, 24/7 work, work for those people who care about us the most and who are therefore the most frightened and tired during this challenging time.

3) Our health care services (insurance, Medicare, Medicaid) do not offer enough comprehensive coverage to address all of the family's in-home care needs--shift coverage being a big uncovered need.

4) Most of us aren't given adequate referral time from our medical professionals to get in-home services in place and support given.

Most people die in the hospital setting. To me, there is nothing comforting about a medical setting. There are rules, protocols, procedures, medical interventions, and certainly no dog or cat on the bed (Although I have been known to smuggle in a cat or two, but that is another story). Hopefully family is given privacy, support of Chaplain services if wanted, and ongoing attention and guidance, but it is still a structured environment.

Another place people can die is in hospice facilities, often called Hospice Houses, which are medical facilities in a home like setting. Staff is trained in end of life care and families have almost total freedom (kitchens to cook in, TV rooms, music room, quiet rooms, sleeping accommodations). A Hospice House is the next best thing to being at home. The family doesn't have the 24/7 responsibility of care, there is a limit to medical disruption, and you can even bring your own dog or cat.

If you say, "Yes, I want to go to a Hospice House," there are two catches: time and money. There is a limited time that you can be in a Hospice House under Medicare coverage. About a week or so is the reimbursed amount unless you switch over to private pay. A good number of us do not have the funds required for several months of private pay.

Which brings us back to dying at home. Hospice in-home services are a great help even with their shift limitations. Hospice care provides families with nursing visits; home health aide visits for bathing and bed changes; medical equipment like beds, wheelchairs, and commodes; counseling and support services; and volunteers to "patient sit" for a few hours of respite for the family caregivers. There is more, I've just named a few offerings. The point I am making is that hospice, when called in earlier than days before death, can set the stage for our "death of choice."

Just like Dorothy says in the Wizard of Oz, "There is no place like home."

The Emperor's New Clothes

Someone asked me to write about "The Emperor's New Clothes." At first I thought it was a prank, and maybe it was, but the question made me wonder how the moral can be applied to end of life care. I came up with a couple of ideas.

At its simplest, Hans Christian Anderson's parable, "The Emperor's New Clothes," tells of an emperor who parades through the streets naked because everyone in the kingdom but one child is too afraid to acknowledge they do not see the Emperor's new clothes.

My first thought is that collective denial can also be an issue with end of life care. Our medical model tells people we can "probably" fix them when, really, a lot of cancers are advanced and not fixable. We provide many forms of chemotherapy, radiation, lab work and multiple procedures aimed at treatment but no one stops to ask what kind of quality of life this treatment will give to the patient. What are the percentages that the treatment will be effective? How much time can we buy with this treatment and at what cost?

Most of us take the treatment, questions unasked, the probabilities not told and then we watch our physical condition deteriorate and wonder why. We remain blind to the naked truth that death is approaching.

My second thought is more of a question: How can we use the power of truth-telling to challenge authority in end of life care? In the last forty years hospice has changed. Hospice started outside of the medical model to address a need that hospitals and medical professionals did not meet. Hospice accepted the fact that death is not a failure of a physician or the medical system but instead a natural occurrence which everyone must eventually face. Hospice recognized that when reasonable treatment has been done and is not effective, truth, comfort, and support are the healing options needed.

During its infancy in the 1970s, hospice concentrated care on the individual and family during approaching death and the actual moment of death. The goal was to be with the family when the patient was actively dying. Today, with all the rules, guidelines, protocols, and governmental micromanagement, the ability of hospice care to meet those early goals is seemingly hindered. We talk of providing comfort care, of support for patient and family, and we do to some degree, but is the naked truth that by being absorbed into the medical model hospice has become too medicalized, using too many medications and doing too many procedures? Are we putting too much emphasis on the physical and too little time on the emotional, mental, and spiritual aspects of dying? In our collective denial about the normalcy of death are we clothing hospice with a medical orientation when the naked truth is that dying is not a medical event but a social, communal event?

As one brave person to another let me know what you think "The Emperor's New Clothes" means for hospice care today.

Section IV: Medical Terminology

Life Sustaining vs. Comfort Care

Question: Life Sustaining vs. Comfort Care: Where Do You Draw the Line?

This is a question everyone faced with a life threatening illness and their significant others asks themselves. We can add to the question, "When do I stop seeking a cure and accept just comfort support?"

I'll begin with the idea that just because the medical establishment can't heal the physical body doesn't mean there isn't healing work left to do. There is still healing of the mental, emotional, and spiritual parts of us that need to be addressed. This is why I say dying isn't a medical event. It is so much more. I will also say that just because we can do a medical procedure doesn't necessarily mean that it is in the best interest of the patient to do it (This topic deserves its own article).

To be clear, let's define cure, life sustaining care, and comfort care.
- A Cure provides a return to a "normal" functioning life (in quotes because normal is a tricky word: whose normal, what is normal, etc.). A cure implies being able to address, partake, and enjoy the activities of living and being alive.
- Life sustaining means keeping the physical body alive in whatever manner that is deemed necessary--including the use of artificial feeding (another whole article), machines (ventilators, dialysis, respirators), and/or advanced medical procedures.
- Comfort Care describes a focus on the quality of life being lived vs. concentrating on the length of that life no matter the quality. Comfort care is good physical body care (address discomforts, hygiene, activity issues); emotional, mental, and spiritual support; addressing what is important to your well being now that your physical body is not meeting your needs; guiding and nurturing those around you that you care about; encouraging you and your family/significant others to live the best you all can within the confines that your body and disease has put you in until you leave your body.

We often get so caught up in getting "fixed" at any price (and I am not just referring to dollars) that we lose sight of what our goal really is. Treatment does not necessarily mean cure. Yet for most of us that is what we are expecting when we do everything possible to stay alive (all too often sacrificing in vain what little quality of life we have left).

For most people with a serious life threatening illness, and by that I mean for those people the doctors are having a difficult time fixing and whose illness is considered "terminal," a cure is unlikely. The question then becomes how much breathing do we want to do when we can't do much else. I know that sounds harsh but I want to get your attention. Most life sustaining treatment is about keeping the lungs, kidneys, and heart functioning--arms, legs, alert thinking, and smiling, not so much.

My step father told me I could have all the life sustaining machines turned off when he had been brain dead for 3 days. He spent the last four months of his life in doctor's offices, in the hospital, or in bed. As the result, he was too sick from treatments to be involved in much interaction around him. Some people want that and we in the medical profession will honor that choice. Some of us will not make that choice.

When it comes to making the decision of cure, life sustaining intervention, or comfort care, I think information and knowledge are vital components to decision making. We need honest information and knowledge about the projected outcomes of treatment, tumor shrinkage, expected life line, and quality of life. Once we have asked these pertinent questions of our physician and stated the direction we want our living to take then we must share that direction with family and significant others as well as to put our directives in writing.

Family will at some point be making the choices about how we will live the rest of our days. If there is no family or signifiant others then the medical profession will make those choices for us UNLESS we have in writing how we want to live until we are dead.

Family members have the most difficult time letting a loved one die. It will never be okay for a mom or dad or anyone close to us to die. We will want them where we can physically see them and touch them, even if that loved one can't respond to us. Selfish, yes, but oh so normal and natural. One of the biggest gifts of love that we can give to our family and to those we care about is to tell them how we want to live until we are dead. Preferably before they need the information.

Terminal Secretions (The Death Rattle)

Death rattle is the scary sound a person often makes in the hours or sometimes days before death. It is fluid that accumulates in the lower throat. The person is not swallowing. The saliva and fluid in the lungs, due to lack of normal body processing (the body is shutting down and nothing works right), is accumulating in the lower part of the throat. That fluid is too deep to really be reached by a suction machine although that is the first thing we think of to get rid of it. The death rattle is not always present. Those people that have more fluid or are more hydrated as they approach death are the ones most likely to experience this natural phenomenon.

Human beings tend to be "fix it" personality types and we particularly expect medical professionals to fix any situation. The death rattle is a normal, natural part of the dying process. It is harder on us, the watchers, than on the person who is dying. By the time a person is experiencing a death rattle they are very much removed from their bodies, generally non responsive, and are busy in the process of letting go of their bodies. The congestion is part of that letting go.

For the "fix it" personalities a Scopolamine Patch is sometimes effective in reducing the secretions as is Atropine 1% drops. Generally, simply repositioning the person from side to side and keeping them off of their back will help reduce the rattle as much as anything. What really helps is that we know that what is happening is very much a part of the normal dying process, that nothing bad is happening. It is scary because we are not used to the sound, it sounds uncomfortable and like it shouldn't be happening so we want it to stop. This is our discomfort. This is part of our fear and grief in the experience. If we understand how the body naturally releases it's hold on life, fear of the experience for us (watching) can be reduced. We can share more comfortably in the gift of being with a loved one who is dying. Our presence at the bedside of love, support, and touch is the comfort that is needed during this last experience of our loved one, not medical intervention.

Terminal Restlessness

Terminal restlessness is a medical term for the restlessness and agitation that often begins one to three weeks before death from disease. The restlessness shows itself by random body movements, hands picking the air or clothing, or by just not being settled and quiet. This restlessness can be from lack of oxygen to the brain but more likely it is just fear showing itself. The body is expressing what it is feeling because the person is beyond expressing itself with words. There are few if any rational conversations now.

To some degree we are all going to be afraid as we approach death. This is normal and natural. Also, we know when we are dying. It is no secret. We live inside of our bodies, we know. In the months before death from disease we don't believe we can't be fixed but there comes a point where we indeed know the time is near (one to three weeks before we actually die from disease). Realizing in the core of our being that we are going to die we become frightened and that fear shows itself in agitation. The belief is, "If I lay down and close my eyes I may die." So we don't lay still, we move about.

Most of the time this restlessness, this agitation, is not destructive. It is not severe. If the movements become thrashing about or hurtful and causing a danger to the person and/or others then a medication to calm is needed. Most people, however, do not need medications for sedation or calming.

Again this activity is normal and natural. It is a part of the dying process from disease or old age. Nothing bad or unusual is happening. The restlessness is just a part of the way we die.

Vomiting

Question: Why didn't you write (in your booklet) about the vomiting that occurred eighteen hours before my husband died?

I am sorry your husband had what appears to be an unusual yet not abnormal experience of vomiting in the hours before he died. I'm sure it was difficult for all of you.

Gone From My Sight: The Dying Experience is a booklet outlining the most common signs of approaching death. Some people will do everything I write about, some people will experience none of the things I write about. Most people experience at least some of the more common signs of approaching death in the months before they die. Because each person dies in their own time and own special way I will not have addressed everything each person does before they die. Again, in an effort to assist the greatest number of varied individuals, I have detailed the most common signs. Vomiting can occur; it is not abnormal if it does. It can happen for a variety of reasons that correspond to the actual disease process of an individual person.

Palliative Sedation

Question: Will you discuss Palliative Sedation?

Palliative sedation is a term used by hospice, palliative care, and medical professionals. The National Hospice and Palliative Care Organization states its position on palliative sedation as follows:

"PALLIATIVE SEDATION - Terminal illnesses can cause distressing symptoms, such as severe pain, mental confusion, muscle spasms, feelings of suffocation, and agitation. Despite skilled palliative care, in some cases these symptoms may not respond to standard interventions. After all other means to provide comfort and relief to a dying patient have been tried and are unsuccessful, doctors and patients can consider palliative sedation. Palliative sedation is the use of sedative medications to relieve extreme suffering by making the patient unaware and unconscious (as in a deep sleep) while the disease takes its course, eventually leading to death. The sedative medication is gradually increased until the patient is comfortable and able to relax. Palliative sedation is not intended to cause death or shorten life." (Vol. 39 No. 5 May 2010 NHPCO Position Statement on the Use of Palliative Sedation 915).

Over the years my personal experience has been that most people who are dying do not need palliative sedation. If pain was not a part of the disease process then the likelihood of pain as death approaches is slim. The actual dying process does not cause pain. It is the particular disease leading a person to death that causes pain. With today's medical advancements there is no reason for a person to die in uncontrolled pain. If the disease process has been a pain filled experience and all comfort management options have been unsuccessful then sleep is our friend. Sleep, created by regulated, supervised medications (palliative sedation), is a compassionate alternative to needless end of life suffering. The key to a gentle death is to relax. If we are in extreme pain and suffering we cannot relax and peacefully leave our bodies.

"People who are dying of a serious medical condition for which no cure is available or for which treatments have failed have a **terminal illness**. These patients can receive comfort care, which focuses not on life-prolonging measures but on relieving pain and suffering at the end of life.

Palliative care provides comfort care to the patient by focusing on relieving symptoms such as pain, anxiety, nausea, and difficulty breathing. Family members as well as the patient are provided with emotional, social, and spiritual support to help them with the dying process.

Hospice care provides palliative treatment, often with a team approach, to serve a variety of patient and family needs such as home nursing care, social services, pain management, and spiritual support. The October 12, 2005, issue of JAMA includes an article about **palliative sedation**." (Oct 12, 2005 Vol. 294, No. 14. Palliative Sedation by Erin Brinder, MD; Alison Burke, MA; Richard M. Glass, MD. JAMA. 2005; 294 (14):1850.doi:10.1001/jama.294.14.1850. http://jama.jamanetwork.com/article.aspx?articleid=201675).

Advance Directives: Afraid to Talk About Dying?

Why are we so afraid to talk about dying, our own or someone else's?

I have a booklet about living with a life threatening illness. It is basically about putting your house in order before you die. It is my least selling booklet, it should be my best.

We are all dying. Life is a terminal illness. Yet we live our lives as if we were immortal hoping to counteract some of these unspoken fears:
- If I talk about dying then I will die.
- If I make plans regarding my death, if I outline my wishes of how I want my dying experience to be, then I will hasten my death.
- If I ignore all end of life issues, they won't happen to me or to my loved ones.

As the result, for one of the biggest, most important experiences of our lives we are the least prepared and therefore the most vulnerable and scared. Whatever happened to the Boy Scout motto, "Be prepared?"

Major religions teach life everlasting; life continues only better. Many religions teach that we will be rewarded for our good endeavors, our good behavior, and our good intentions. If the above is what we truly believe and have practiced in our living then why do we hold on to this life so fiercely? In part because we don't want to leave what we do know and because we are afraid of what we don't know.

Even though our religions teach a belief about the after life, how do we really know it is true? We don't, yet I don't think that questioning is a sign of weakness in our belief system but more of an acknowledgment of our humanness.

Facing our mortality is a courageous act. It is a mature, thoughtful act and although it places us outside of our comfort zone of denial it provides guidance for those we leave behind. It relieves those we care about from making decisions for us that they may wrestle with for the rest of their lives. Facing our own mortality, having a Living Will (a document that states in advance a person's end of life wishes), assigning a Medical Durable Power of Attorney (a document that gives a person of your choosing the legal authority to make medical decisions for you if and when you are unable to make those decisions yourself), making our wishes known in regard to how we want to experience our final act of living, is one of the greatest gifts of love we can give to those we care about.

Link to a free download of an Advance Directive: lifecaredirectives.com/statutory.html

Full Code vs. No Code

Question: How do you help someone convert from a full code to a no code?

I think the best way to help with the full code/no code decision is to educate people. I'll begin with basic definitions. A "full code" means that if your heart stops (and you have died), the medical professionals in a hospital or paramedics from a 911 phone call will do everything medically possible to try and restart the heart. A "no code" means if your heart stops (and you have died), the medical professionals in a hospital or paramedics from a 911 call, will NOT try to restart your heart. They will let a person stay dead.

This sounds very harsh so lets explore this idea further. We are conditioned to think that a call to 911 can help us no matter what the emergency is and to think that the doctors, while we are in the hospital, will always be able to "fix us." Because everyone dies, whether or not we want to admit it, there will come a point when the medical system will "fail" us. It will be our time to die. When the doctors have said, "I can't fix you" it is time to reconsider what medicine can do for us. Medicine can prolong life but generally at the expense of our well being. Or we can consider using medicine only as a tool to provide comfort, dignity, and support as our final life experience unfolds.

If I stuck my finger in a light socket and my heart stopped, I would want you to call 911. The paramedics could probably restart my heart and I would return to my normal life and activities.

If my body is filled with a disease that the doctors have said they cannot fix, my heart stops, and I do not have a No Code order or DNR (Do Not Resuscitate) form completed, the paramedics or doctors are bound by their profession to try to start my heart again. And they may succeed BUT in most cases I will not be as able as I was before my heart stopped and my disease will still be non-fixable. I will just have to die again in a short time. In that short time there will be continued decline of my body, continued progress of the disease, the pain will remain--may even be increased due to the resuscitation efforts-- and my life will have less and less quality.

Section V: Grief

Normal Grief

I'm going to talk about normal, natural grief and break it into a brief, manageable size. Visualize a table in front of an open window. There are stacks of paper on the table; tidy, organized stacks. A slight breeze comes through the window and rustles the papers. Now a strong wind comes through and scatters the papers everywhere.

The above image is what grieving is like. Some days you do just fine, have it all together. Other days you feel restless, uneasy but go about your day. Then some days you can't even get out of bed without crying. You look through pictures and the best you can do is have a crying, I feel sorry for myself day. The next day, you brush yourself off and begin again.

Grief is a lot of emotions rolled into one package. Grief from the griever's perspective is:

- **I'm sad and lonely** because you are not in my life anymore. My loneliness is the result of isolation. That isolation is two fold: One, I don't have the energy to reach out to others for support, comfort, or in friendship. Two, because others tend to stay away from me. Others are uncomfortable around me because they don't know what to say. Others are afraid they might say something that will make me feel worse.
- **I am confused and adrift.** My life has changed and I don't know where to start or what to do to create a new one. My direction and focus in life has to be different now.
- **I'm angry.** I liked my life the way it was. Everything was great and then you died. Now you are gone and I have to change. I'm angry about that. I'm angry with you for dying. You're gone and I am the one who has to deal with everything. I'm the one that has to start over. I'm angry with God for letting this happen. Why did this happen to me? Oh, I had better not tell anyone how angry I am. I believe people will think I am a bad person so I hold the anger inside of me and become depressed.
- **I'm so depressed.** My anger held inward becomes depression. I'm so depressed I can't leave the house, some days I can't even get dressed. I can't eat or I eat too much. I can't sleep or I sleep too much. I am so depressed.
- **I'm frightened.** We did everything we were supposed to do. We ate the right foods, exercised, did all the right treatments, and you died anyway. I am not as in control of my life as I thought I was. These feelings tell me I and others close to me could die too. Death takes away the idea that we are immortal. This realization is frightening.
- I'm **sad**, I'm **lonely**, I'm **isolated**, I'm **confused** and **adrift**, I'm **angry**, I'm **depressed**, and I'm **scared**. All of these start with I. Grief is very self centered. It is not about the person who has died. It is how we are feeling about the situation life has put us in. I don't mean this in a negative way. It is just how it is.

Most religious belief systems teach that when you are dead you are in a better place. If we hold that belief then we are not worried about the person who has died. They are better off than we are. Living is hard work, being dead is easy. I point this out because most of us think our feelings, our grief, is about the person who died. It is not. It is about us, about how our life has to change, and how we are going to adapt to those changes.

We don't heal from grief. We don't recover from grief. We learn how to live with grief. Our life will never be the same again but time will begin to fill in the space between the pain that we feel over our loss.

Grieving and Suicide

Question: How do you grieve a suicide as a result of terminal illness and for no apparent reason?

But there is a reason and that reason is the terminal illness. The suicidal thoughts and resulting end of life is about being afraid of what the coming months will hold, of actually being more afraid of the experience leading up to death than death itself. The thought is, "If I am going to be dying soon then let's just skip over the dying part, that really scares me, and let me be dead."

Sometimes it is just too hard to go on living. The future looks too bleak and scary so we end our life earlier than most expected of us. Look to the person's personality, to how they have dealt with other challenges in their life. Have they run away from other life challenges? Suicide is the ultimate "runaway." Although I think it takes a great deal of courage to kill yourself it often takes more courage to live until we die.

How do you grieve this sudden loss? Painfully, and with questions to which you will never find answers. All the "what ifs", "why didn't I", and "I should haves" will fill our grieving brain and make our grieving even more difficult than it normally would be.

In our grief we have to forgive ourselves for what might have been if only-----. Those self recriminations accomplish nothing but making us more miserable. They answer no questions, bring no peace.

There are no words that I can offer you to make you feel better in your grief. Time will ease the pain but even that knowledge is not comforting to hear. Be gentle with yourself, forgive what needs to be forgiven of yourself and others, release the questions that have no answers and let the life you live be your tribute to the loved one who is gone.

Grieving and Dementia

Question: Please talk about grieving the gradual but sure loss of a loved one with dementia.

Perhaps you've heard it said, "Having a loved one with dementia is the long goodbye." We lose the person we know long before their body dies. As with all terminal illness, grief begins with the diagnosis--for the the patient, as well as everyone close to them. For someone who can't be fixed there is a gradual progression of disease which ends in death. For someone with dementia, because the mind goes in advance of the body, our loved one gradually becomes a person we really don't know. Not knowing our loved one becomes not knowing how to interact with them. "Who is this woman who is my mother? I don't know her and she doesn't know me. What do we do with each other?"

As the person gradually changes and becomes less able to function mentally and emotionally, we, the watchers, must adjust because the person with dementia can't even fathom what is occurring. We, the watchers, must learn to accept our loved one not for who they used to be but who and where they are now. This is part of our grieving.

Memories are made of the past and hopes are part of the future. People with dementia force those of us around them to live in the present--what is occurring right now is what is important, is what is happening. With memory loss the past is gone and the future is not contemplated, only the present has value.

Grief for the dead is self centered. Most of us believe the deceased is in a better place so our grief is about us (the living) having to adjust to what we have lost.

Grief for a person with dementia is for the afflicted as well as for ourselves, for all that has been and is being lost.

Grief for the dead allows us to move forward, to make a new life built on positive, balanced memories.

Grief for a person with dementia holds us in place, prevents us from moving on, from rebuilding. Everyday we are reminded just by being in their presence what we have lost and are still losing.

My only remedy for the ongoing grief experienced by the caregiver of a person with Alzheimer's, or any other form of dementia, is love and acceptance. Acceptance for who our loved one is and what they can do today. Acceptance that they are unable to consciously give us what we want from them, as a spouse, as a child, as a sibling. Acceptance that we no longer have a give and take relationship. However, we can give to them. We can give love, give acceptance, and give presence. We can ask for nothing, just give and see what happens. And we need to give the same love and acceptance we offer our loved one to ourselves as we go through this challenging experience of continuous grief.

All this said, I know I have not addressed the hostility, anger, and aggression that can occur. These facets of a changing personality can hurt and bewilder us. I can only suggest we gently remind ourselves not to take these effects of our loved one's disease personally (easier said than done) and to continually separate the current behavior from the memory of the relationship. Try to love the person and the memory, not the behavior.

Many books have been written about how to live with the tragedy of dementia. What is written here just touches upon the body of knowledge available today to guide and support those of us faced with this complex experience.

Family and Grief

Question: Explain the different ways members of the same family experience grief.

Grief is a lot of emotions rolled into one package. Each person will experience and show these emotions in their own way and own time. When we are grieving we may all have the same emotions and often we have the same thoughts but we will show them differently because each of us is a unique individual. As a family, members may be experiencing different feelings at different times.

Grief can show itself in physical ailments. Grief physically hurts. You can feel tired and listless.

Grief is the feeling I am sad and lonely because you are not in my life anymore.

Grief is the feeling I am confused and adrift. My life has changed and I don't know where to start or what to do to create a new one. I can't seem to think clearly.

Grief is the feeling I am angry. I'm angry with you for dying. You're gone and I'm the one who has to start over. I'm angry with God for letting this happen. Why did this happen to me? Often people are unable to express their anger so they find fault with others or become argumentative, or just hold the anger in and not express it but it is under the surface of their life and actions.

Grief is the feeling I am so depressed. Anger held inward becomes depression. I am so depressed I can't leave the house, some days I can't even get dressed. I can't eat or I eat too much. I can't sleep or I sleep too much. I am so depressed.

Grief is the feeling I am frightened. I am not as in control of my life as I thought I was. We did everything we were supposed to do. We ate the right foods, exercised, did all the right treatments and you died anyway. These feelings tell me I and others close to me could die too. Death takes away the idea that we are immortal. This realization is frightening.

We can have all these feelings at once or one at a time. They will come and go. Some days will be easier than others.

Grief and the Holidays

Our seasonal holidays are here and for those of us who have had loved ones die this year the holidays will be a particularly challenging time. Something to think about: We tend to play the "elephant in the room" game regarding the mention of our missing loved one. "If we don't talk about how sad we are feeling we won't spoil the day for others" is a common belief we carry into group gatherings. The fallacy in this kind of thinking is that everyone is sad and missing this special person and they are all thinking the same about each other. SO, bring those feelings out into the open and share them, right at the beginning of the get together: "It just isn't going to be the same this year without Mom," "Who is going to carve the turkey now that Dad is not here?"

Another idea is to actually plan on including the person in the day. Since so much of our celebrating involves meals, reserve a place at the table, maybe put a picture instead of a plate and silverware in the reserved spot. Talk openly about him or her. Have each person present say what is in their heart as you go around the table before or after eating. The idea is to be open with everyone about the loss you are experiencing. Share stories and reminisce, get out the scrapbooks, cry, laugh, and support one another. Your loved one will not be there physically but their spirit will be kept alive and cherished.

When is it Time to Say Goodbye?

Question: When is it time to say goodbye?

There is a saying, "Live each day as if it were your last." It makes sense that the last day of our lives is the day we would want to say goodbye. Unfortunately, on our last day we probably won't be able to say goodbye. If we are dying a gradual death from disease we will be non responsive. If it is a fast death those people who mean the most to us probably won't be with us.

SO--when is it time to say goodbye? Everyday! Live each day so that at the end of it there are no regrets, no unfinished business, and nothing that will create guilt feelings later.

The above is actually my life philosophy. I really think the person who asked the question was referring to when do we say our final goodbye to someone who is dying. I believe we say our goodbye in stages.

Ideally, we have expressed our appreciation for the relationship and our goodbyes in the months to weeks before death actually occurs. We have an intimate conversation when the person who is dying is still alert and interacting with us. Later, in the hours to minutes before death when the person is non responsive, we say goodbye again. It is easier to talk to a person who is non responsive, to say everything our heart tells us to say. This is the goodbye where you talk about the difficult times as well as the good times, a cleaning of the slate so to speak.

Another goodbye is said after the person we care about is dead. This is done at the bedside before the body is taken to the mortuary or at the coffin. This goodbye is said out loud or within your heart.

Then there is a final goodbye. I recommend we write a letter to put all of our thoughts on paper. Write about the relationship, positive and challenging, write about love, forgiveness, and understanding. Whatever is in your heart that still needs to be said, write it down. That letter can go into the coffin (under the hands, pillow, or wherever you feel comfortable placing it) or, if there is no coffin, do something special with the letter. Keep the letter in a special place, burn it and release the ashes to the wind, or put it over flowers in a garden. Do something special with it.

When is the time to say goodbye? Many, many, times.